نمبر کہانی

THE NUMBER STORY

SMALL BOOK ONE

ENGLISH - URDU

Numbers Teach Children
Their Number Names

written and illustrated by

MISS ANNA

Early Reader Edition of *The Number Story 1*
Bronze Medal Winner, 2016 Wishing Shelf Book Award

Library of Congress Control Number: 2018902040

Names: Miss Anna, author.
Title: Number story : numbers teach children their number names / Miss Anna.
Description: Portland, OR: Lumpy Publishing, 2018.
Identifiers: ISBN 978-1-945977-53-4 | LCCN 2018902040
Summary: The pictures and rhymes present stories which introduce numbers 0-10.
Subjects: LCSH Numeration—English--Urdu--Pictorial works--Juvenile literature. | BISAC JUVENILE NONFICTION /
Languages: English--Urdu
Classification: LCC QA141.3 .M57 2018 | DDC 513—dc23

Publisher: Lumpy Publishing
Website: www.missannabooks.com
Email: missanna@missannabooks.com

Paperback: ISBN 978-1-945977-53-4
Printed in the U.S.A.   1 3 5 7 9 10 8 6 4 2

Want to learn our number names?

ہمارے نام سیکھنا چاہتے ہیں؟

It is very easy and a lot of fun!

یہ بہت آسان اور بہت مزیدار ہے!

Say-along our little jingle

آو ساتھ مل کے گائیں۔

starting from Number One!

آو نمبر ایک سے شروع کریں!

1

ONE looks like my one finger.

١ ایک

ایک میری انگلی ہے۔

ONE!
ایک

2

TWO trails a tail.

۲ دو

دو کی پونچھ ہے .

A TAIL!

ایک پونچھ!

3

THREE has bumps.

۳ تین

تین پہاڑ کی طرح ہے۔

پہاڑوں کی طرف دیکھ!

4

ایک کشتی!

5

FIVE   is a racing track.

٥ پانچ

پانچ ایک ریسنگ ٹریک ہے .

VROOM
وروم !

6

SIX curves like a snail.

٦ چھ

چھ گھونگے کی طرح گول ہے۔

A SNAIL!

ایک گھونگا!

7

SEVEN   has a sharp angle.

۷ سات

سات کی دھار ہے۔

OUCH!
BE CAREFUL!
محتاط رہیں!

8
EIGHT   is rollercoaster rails.
۸ ⋆ آٹھ
آٹھ رولر کوسٹر ہیں۔

!
YIPPEE!

NINE   is a bubble on a stick.

A BUBBLE!
ایک بلبلا!

TEN   is an eye of a whale.

دس ایک وہیل کی آنکھ ہے۔

HELLO!
هيلو !

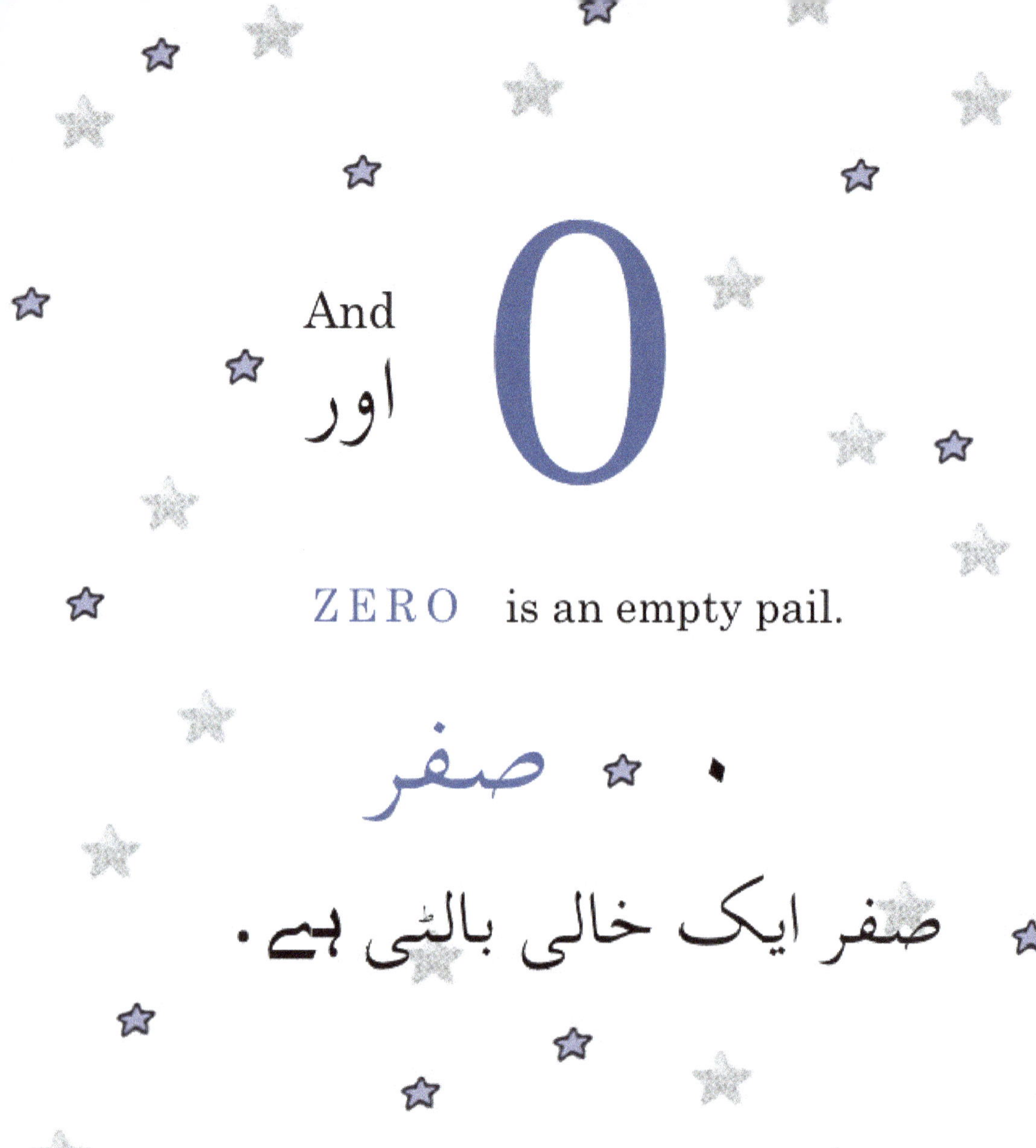
And اور O

ZERO   is an empty pail.

۰ صفر

صفر ایک خالی بالٹی ہے۔

IT'S EMPTY!
خالی ہے !

Thank you for playing with us today.

We had a lot of fun too!

ہمارے ساتھ کھیلنے کے لئے شکریہ!

ہمیں بہت مزہ آیا!

We are your Number friends,
Zero to Ten,
Who will be here for you~

ہم نمبر آپ کے دوست ہیں
صفر سے دس تک۔
ہم ہمیشئہ آپ کے ساتھ ہوں گے!

Bye-bye now!
See you again soon.

خدا حافظ!
بہت جلد دوبارہ ملیں گے!

The Numbers are *SINGING* too!

To sing-a-long, look for Miss Anna Number Story
at your favorite music store like iTUNES.

MP3

Numbers 0-10
IDENTIFYING
& COUNTING

Numbers 11-20
& Ordinals

first, second, third...

Numbers 0-100
& Place Values

ones, tens, hundreds...

About Clock
& Telling Time

hours, minutes, seconds

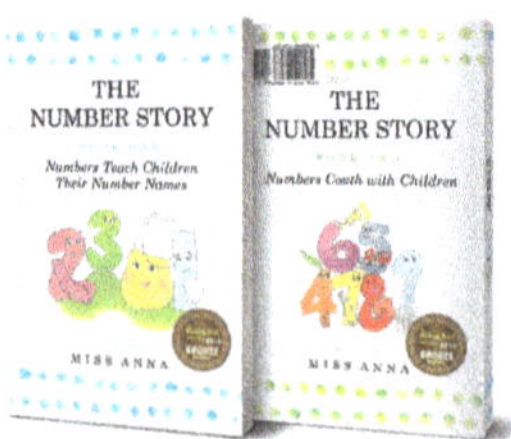

Number Story 1 & 2

isbn: 978-0-996216-48-7

Number Story 3 & 4

isbn: 978-1-945977-01-5

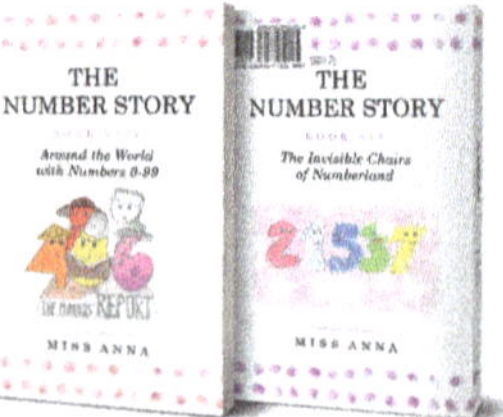

Number Story 5 & 6

isbn: 978-1-945977-06-0

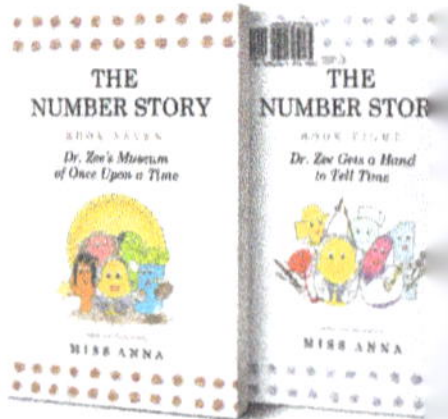

Number Story 7 & 8

isbn: 978-1-949320-4

For more Miss Anna books to love,
visit us at

www.missannabooks.com

Numbers are working hard all over the world!
Come Travel the World with Us!